Out of the Box

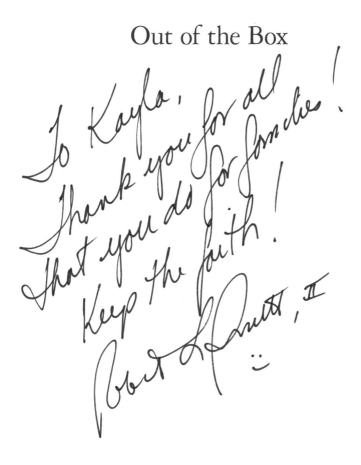

To Kayla,
Thank you for all
that you do for families!
Keep the faith!
Robert L. Pruitt, II
:)

Visit www.booksurge.com to order additional copies.

ROBERT LEIGH
PRUITT II

OUT OF THE BOX

SHARING THE GIFT YOU ARE WITH THE WORLD!

2007

Out of the Box

CONTENTS

To My Father, Who At The End Of Life Showed Me How To Live And Focus On God And My Mother, Who Is My Greatest Fan And Continues To Model Faith In God, Resilience, Laugher And Love.

PROLOGUE

Each one should use whatever gift he has received to serve others...

—1 Peter 4:10

The first movie I remember enjoying at an early age was the *Wizard of Oz*. Each time I saw the movie, I feared Dorothy's nasty neighbor, Ms. Gulch, who rode off with Toto trapped in a wooden basket on the back of her bicycle. My eyes opened wide as the tornado spun the farm house around. And I peeked through my fingers when the house landed on the witch and her striped stockings curled up like a party favor.

I loved the energy of the Good Witch and the Munchkins. The Yellow Brick Road was great because it took me on Dorothy's journey. It was on that magical road that I was introduced to the Scarecrow, Tin-Man, and Cowardly Lion, the haunted forest, the poppy field and the Emerald City. I cringed when the great and powerful Oz spoke in his deep ominous voice; I felt sick watching the sand in the witch's hour glass run out wondering what would happen to Dorothy if it did; I was horrified when the witch melted away; and I celebrated when the diploma, the heart shaped clock; and the medal of honor were awarded to Dorothy's friends; Surprise and fear gripped me when the hot air balloon left without Dorothy;

and I wondered why the Good Witch waited until the end of the movie to tell Dorothy she had the power to go home at any time.

Like Dorothy, we are all on some kind of a journey. Many people have returned from "Oz" and know, first hand, the power of *thinking* a new way, *stepping* through life in a different manner, and *discovering* something new about themselves and their power to positively impact their world. For these risk takers the world is seen as bright, colorful, full of life and ripe with endless possibilities. And they would never have generated this new perception if the "Good Witch" (spiritual force, parent, friend, or mentor) in their lives had given them the "answer" at the beginning of their journey.

There are, however, some people who figuratively still remain in "Kansas or even stuck in the Land of Oz." I identify with this experience. I wasted the time and gifts given to me by God. I buried my treasures in the ground and tried to keep my light from shining brightly. I viewed life as a dusty, dismal existence (as Kansas was depicted in the beginning of the movie) where I merely went through the motion of existing each day. It was a routine life that I had created for myself, yet I silently dreamt of changing it. I desired to live a life full of promise—a life somewhere over the rainbow.

I met people along this journey who, like me, talked about change but rarely committed to it; however, I was astonished, and at the same time impressed, by those who actually created the results they envisioned. And I'm not speaking of people who accumulated great wealth. I'm highlighting individuals who dedicated their life to serving others and in doing so let their light shine. I'm talking about people who continuously faced their fears in an effort to share the gift they were created to be with the world. From watching these people, I realized:

1) it was possible to make my dreams come true, 2) people break their habits at different rates, 3) many of us do not realize that happiness and enlightenment (purpose) comes through service to others, 4) no matter what my situation, there is always an opportunity to light someone else's candle, 5) a life of significance (loving and being loved by others) matters more to me than a life marked by material success (cars, fancy clothes, and jewelry) and 6) someone bigger than "man" was in control.

My lack of self-awareness caused me to blame others for my life. I felt that I needed to blame something (job, school, society) or someone else (girlfriend, parent, friend) for my ordinary, boring, lackluster, painful existence. I was literally taking up space in the world and producing little of substance and value. This negatively impacted my spiritual life and arrested my personal development.

How often do you want to blame the Gulchs of the world for your thoughts, emotional state, actions, or miserable results rather than holding yourself accountable and choosing to do something different? *Blame* is defined as the absence of personal responsibility. And when we believe our own lies and do the same thing the same way, expecting a different result, we've just defined *insanity*.

At the beginning of the movie, a field hand tells Dorothy that she possesses the power to end the ongoing feud with Mrs. Gulch. When Dorothy ignores this advice and continues to allow Toto to roam freely, she is "stuck on stupid." She maintains the same behavior and then complains that the punishment is unfair. Could Dorothy's behavior be a cry for attention? Possibly, but that does not absolve her from being held accountable and responsible for her actions.

We know Dorothy secretly desired more than a ho-hum life. This is confirmed when she runs away from home and seeks the wisdom of a carnival mystic. When the mystic reminds Dorothy of the importance of family love, she fights her way through the storm to return home. Upon her arrival, the young girl discovers the locked storm doors and is metaphorically shut out of her family's life again. Alone, frighten, vulnerable, and disconnected, Dorothy's world seems to twist around her.

Caught up in the *intrapersonal* (how she views herself) and *interpersonal* (how she relates to others) winds of change, Dorothy is provided with another chance to discover what matters to her. But to achieve this, she would have to break free of her insanity and live way outside her comfort zone. Have you ever run to family or friends to escape being responsible for your life only to be told that running away is not the answer?

It was through this story that it became clearer to me that the supreme being, whom I call God, endows us all with gifts and requires that we faithfully use our gifts to make a difference in the world (1 Peter 4:10). It was also clear that if life is to be the way we want, it's up to each of us to create that life by using our gifts. However, not all of us use our gifts to serve others. Some use their gifts for personal gain. Others, like Dorothy, may not realize that they have gifts to share. Our talents, skills, and experiences mean little if we don't take the time to envision what we can create with them. Our visions will not materialize if we don't identify our gifts and put them to use (Romans 12: 6-8).

If you flew over a rainbow, right now, to the land of purpose and peace, what would you discover matters to you: a world without famine; a world free from bigotry; a place where kids can play free from predators; a world devoid of family, sexual and substance abuse? Would supportive relationships, more money, less stress, or greater insight into who you are be of primary concern?

This book is designed to support you in declaring and creating and (re)committing yourself to the life you are destined to live. It's not a substitute for counseling nor is it "church" in a book. Rather it seeks to be a spiritual aide for moving you from generating excuses to doing what matters. It's about developing healthy relationships with the Supreme Being, yourself, significant others, siblings, children, peers, co-workers and the communities that need you to serve them in that order. It's about sharing the gift you are more often, with fewer attachments or conditions.

I've found that every day I either nurture and maintain, or tear down my self-image and my relationships. The establishment of healthy relationships is contingent upon knowing ourselves coupled with a willingness to disclose this knowledge and alter our behavior. The willingness to share ourselves, coupled with the desire to accept others for who they are, builds trust and creates intimacy. This strengthens relationships.

Who we are is a function of how we see ourselves. Seeing ourselves in the likeness of God defines us as loving, compassionate, forgiving, powerful and faithful. If we see ourselves in the likeness of humans, we tend to take on those characteristics. This means we tend to create a self-image that reflects our relationships. This can have both benefits and drawbacks. For example, in Kansas, Dorothy's guardians spent more time tending to the needs of the farm then they did to the needs of the young girl. As a result, Dorothy became aloof and distant, seeing herself as insignificant. However, when Dorothy met the Good Witch (who represents for me a spiritual force), her attitude and behaviors changed and so did the view she held of herself. She became wise, loving and courageous. What we offer to others is a product of the view we hold of ourselves.

I am constantly reminded of how much our interpretation of a childhood experience shapes our lives. For years, I believed my results defined me. I put my trust and faith in the products or results I created. But, one experience changed all that. I remember sitting in 7th-grade Latin class waiting for the teacher to arrive. She entered the room, turned off the lights and instructed us to clear our desks. She then sat down on her desk and took out a ring suspended on a thick silver necklace. "Class," she said, "you have the power to make this chain do what you want." I thought she had lost it. She asked two students to hold her wrists while she let the chain hang from her fingers. The teacher instructed the class to think about the chain moving clock-wise. Within seconds the chain began moving. "It's moving," a fellow student shouted. She told us to think about creating bigger circles. We were in disbelief. I was in even greater shock when the two students holding her wrists said the teacher wasn't moving or breathing on the necklace. We made the chain swing out wide, slow down and even switch directions. However, when the chain jumped up and down, the class was speechless. That's when she told us to put our heads on the desk, close our eyes, and spend the rest of the period saying, "I am an 'A' student."

We began each class silently repeating our affirmation. My grades jumped from D- to B's and A's. When I transferred schools, I took that lesson with me. My grades continued to improve and I eventually earned a spot on the honor roll. Before that magical experience in Latin class, I told myself I was stupid when I received an "F" on a test. Once I created this belief, I naturally acted in a way (not studying or completing assignments) that would produce consistent results: a failing grade. I've discovered that we are creatures of habit, and sabotage was one of many bad habits. In recent years, I've discovered my results are simply feedback that tells me how I'm doing relative to my goal. The goal is whatever I make it: gaining freedom, eradicating violence, or sharing openly. Today, I use my results to measure where I am in life rather than to define who I am. When I make a mistake, I am more likely to say "I made a mistake, and I am capable of doing something differently." Please know that doing something differently doesn't mean things will be "better," nor does it guarantee a successful outcome.

In addition, I have found that in choosing to be an authentic, committed, courageous, loving, forgiving, respectful, nurturing, supportive and protective being, that I have created a standard of excellence for my life. This standard is also how I measure my actions. In the past, I got caught up in trying to live by someone else's ideal of me. Romans 12:2 says, *"Don't copy the behavior and customs of this world, but let God transform you into a new person by changing the way you think. Then you will know what God wants you to do, and you will know how good and pleasing and perfect his will really is."*

It wasn't until I stopped running from God that I began to hold myself accountable for my life and its effect on others. Before he died of cancer, my father, the 103rd Bishop of the African Methodist Episcopal Church, told me to "let go of the anger and be God's man." These words stung. It wasn't what I wanted to hear, but it was what I needed to hear. Those nine words hit the core of my being and called me to take responsibility for my life. My father never preached long, but this had to have been the shortest and most effective sermon ever. Thanks to Dad, I've discovered that being responsible fosters self-respect, and that produces a healthy self-image. Gaining respect for myself and the world around me supports me in searching for the gift in others. Prior to this, I only looked for what was wrong with people and the world. Today, Kansas not only looks different, it *is* different. You too have the power to click your heels, (re)discover your authentic self and see your world as beautiful and full of possibilities.

The chapters in this book are short and provide activities to facilitate deeper connections between the readings and your experiences. I've also provided a few tools that you can use as you travel down your path. We'll journey through a few of the thoughts, emotions and actions that produce tears of joy and tears of pain. We'll use T.E.A.R.'s as a life tool. This acronym stands for "thoughts" "emotions" "actions" and "results" and helps to identify how we are operating [See Chapter 3].

There's no right or wrong way to use this book. However, I have a few suggestions to help maximize the potential for breakthrough (i.e. spiritual enlightenment). First, I invite you to pray for understanding before each reading. Second, skim through the book without completing any of the exercises. Simply get a feel for the book. Then go back and immerse yourself in each chapter and complete the activities. Third, take notes in the margins, or keep a journal entitled, "What I've Discovered is…" Finally, use a Bible as a reference. I don't want you to walk away with "Robert's thoughts." Rather I want you to be guided to God's absolute wisdom through my writing. If you find yourself resisting your efforts to move through this book, create small achievable steps (i.e., read one or two paragraphs). Focus on the quality of your experience rather than how quickly you move through the book. If you find yourself in 'breakdown' and in need of support, click your heels and contact me: Robert@robertpruitt.com or www. robertpruitt.com or 866-766-5323(LEAD).

It has taken several years and many prayerful rewrites to complete this book. And even now, I pray God's *will* be done. I know first hand how difficult we can make life. And not consciously including God in my life has been costly. There are still times when I succumb to fear, let go of His hand and hide in my box. However, I've found it impossible to hide from myself. My vision to help people understand their significance and live to serve others doesn't occur when I lock myself away. My father said, "Faith is always mixed with doubt." And, I'm sure we're all destined to have numerous "in the box" moments. You will no doubt find times when you choose to spend too much time in your comfort zone. My prayer is that you will ask the Father to deliver you from your self-imposed container. Remind yourself that "*You are a gift*," and that gifts are to be shared. So, as you continue to serve, lead and love, keep God first and continue to keep the faith!

Life should be about living in excellence. Excellence makes room for mistakes and breakdowns. Breakdowns provide opportunities to gain insight and wisdom. Life is not just about us. It's about the good that we seek to do for others with the talents and time we've been given. Life is short, how long are you going to wait to be great? Each day calls for urgent, focused action. Someone, somewhere in our world needs you to "breakthrough" today so they will see God in you and know that their "Kansas" can be different.

CHAPTER 1
What Does the "Box" Represent?

My life is worth nothing unless I use it for doing the
work assigned me by the Lord Jesus.

Acts 20:24

The box is simply a metaphor for our lives. It's also called our "comfort zone." Our box, our body, is the temporary container from which we operate our lives. It holds everything that makes up who we are today as well as the information that governs our daily behaviors. The box is the place we go when we feel confident or when we feel threatened.

I realized how this worked after separating from my first wife in 1995. Until then, I hadn't looked at the behaviors that contaminated all of my relationships. I had been critical and judgmental of everyone and everything and, to top it off, selfish. I believed it was "the entire world against me," and if I didn't matter to the world, then others didn't matter to me. This, of course, wasn't how I really felt. Deep inside, I felt threatened. My attitude served as my defense mechanism—my attempt to justify my behavior—a way to remain inside the box and continue to take from the world.

At that point, I realized my marriage was a relationship of convenience for me. I was not living my life to the fullest.

Instead, I was attempting to create a complete life through marriage. I used someone in an effort to feel complete, significant, and secure. But I was far from comfortable. I was safe in my box and not building a healthy self image or healthy relationships. In fact, much of what I gave to all my relationships was superficial. I didn't share much about myself because I didn't know much.

It wasn't until I disclosed my "true" feelings (as I understood them at that time) with my first wife that I started stepping out of the box. Living a lie was not healthy. I could not continue to hurt people and a change was needed. After a sporadic courtship of five years that culminated in a wedding only 15 months earlier, I decided to end the fledgling marriage.

Several months and a few counseling sessions later, I recognized my "box." My counselor helped me discover its contents. Until then, I had been unwilling to identify who I had been (rude, selfish), what I had offered (lies, alienation), who I wanted to be (loving, confident), and what I had to offer to the world (support, the gift of speech).

It became clear to me that "the box" is the gift that is "you." Opening it reveals the "authentic you." In revealing the authentic self, we give others the best gift we have to offer— our full and complete selves. When we freely give ourselves to others, we create opportunities to build healthy, nurturing, protective relationships, families, and communities. Strong relationships require that we identify the healthy things in our box, and take a look at those things that we can put in "storage." Then we must be willing to continuously risk and step outside of what is familiar, comfortable, and predictable to access something new.

You see, our box is equipped with walls that serve as barriers protecting its precious contents. When events threaten us, our comfort zone protects us from pain, disappointment, and extreme discomfort. When the walls become barriers that conceal our true emotions from others, our personal and collective growth is stunted. Many times we succeed in convincing others that we are happy with our life. We hide behind the "fake" self and never feel exposed. It is our way of controlling our experience of life. We sabotage our relationship with self and others because we fear rejection, disapproval, or disappointment. Many of us close the lid to our box—shutting the world out, and our lies and deception in.

This realization was the beginning of a scary yet extraordinary journey down my yellow brick road. I finally decided to take responsibility for defining who I was, and took ownership of my life. My relationships changed instantly. I started by apologizing to those closest to me for not being honest and sharing with them what I wanted from my relationship with them. I even revived my childhood dreams to travel the United States and visit Europe. Within twelve months I had driven across the country and visited England and France. A year later I returned to England and journeyed to West Africa.

I no longer had to hope that someone in Oz could give me the life I desired. I simply began clicking my heels and the dreams that I dared to dream really did come true. However, there was still a lot to learn about the contents of my box. And there were more anxious times ahead.

In the *Wizard of Oz*, Dorothy did not realize that she was responsible for shutting her family and friends out of her life. Like Dorothy, I discovered that my *thoughts* generated *emotions* and those emotions governed my *actions*. Those actions always produced *results* [We'll discuss T.E.A.R.'s in Chapter 3.] Aligning my desires with God's will provided numerous opportunities to travel and serve. In my travels, I have met people who either do not understand or have forgotten that they create their dull, disconnected, seemingly insignificant life.

This was true when I traveled to India in 2004 to conduct my Strengthen Your Foundation leadership program with 100 leaders from a Fortune 500 company. The common thought that ran through these extraordinarily beautiful people was they felt insignificant or doomed to live a routine existence.

Similarly, Dorothy felt insignificant in Kansas. As a result of this thinking, she ran away in an effort to find love and acceptance (i.e., happiness). The result? Her family thought she was gone and they had to choose between looking for Dorothy in the midst of a storm and seeking shelter (a choice Dorothy knew nothing about). Dorothy never openly expressed: 1) that she loved her family, and 2) that she needed them to express their love in a way that she understood. Instead, Dorothy assumed she knew the "truth" about her family's feelings. Her assumptions created the belief that happiness could only be found away from home.

Let me be clear about the type of assumption I mean here. If, for example, you are in an abusive relationship, assuming you would be happier somewhere else may be healthy and beneficial. Conversely, there are times we assume that others will hurt us, and we run away from or sabotage those relationships without testing the assumption. Dorothy created her own pain, yet believed her actions would prevent others from hurting her. In cases like this, we do unto ourselves before others do unto us and then blame the world for our pain. This lack of personal responsibility stunts our growth. Where there is limited or no growth there is little understanding of the self. When we don't gain new insight into who we are and what we have to offer, we have less to share. In some cases we stop opening up—resulting in superficial or forced conversations.

For the group in India, their self defeating assumptions about working with other departments within the company shut down inter-departmental creativity and limited their conversations to a perfunctory, "hello," "goodbye," and "it's just another day." Don't get me wrong, the group genuinely respected each other, but their interactions had become predictable and flat.

One hour into the first day of a three-day program, they traveled over the rainbow and began to reconnect with their gifts and each other. On day two, the room was full of laughter and curiosity. On the final day, they admitted to an awakening of the spirit. They were now eager to take full responsibility for their teams. A week after returning to the States I received the following email:

Dear Mr. Robert

At the outset, let me thank you and my management for providing one of the very best three days of my life to date.—The high point of the workshop according to me was on the 2nd and 3rd day, i.e. "Mastery of Love" and "Mastery of Transformation."

—The commitment level you maintained and the determination (even though away from home) which I saw in you from the word go, very much impressed me and no doubt you are living your VISION. These qualities are the Hallmark of great achievers and outstanding professionals and I pray that I follow your suit and achieve my goals and contribute more to others, be it my company, my home or friends...

—The workshop had given me an excellent time and opportunity for making self-examination and opened several undiscovered attributes from my box which I could now concentrate on. It's time to say goodbye, as I start to live my Vision in the best possible manner.

I admire you Mr. Robert for all your concern for the underprivileged and may we all work to help them in whatever capacity we can for their betterment. I have to say you have really "strengthened my foundation."

This program participant chose to stand and face his "undiscovered attributes." Many others choose to avoid conflict rather than work though the discomfort associated with personal growth. Many times we run from our own inability or unwillingness to be assertive. One of my greatest lessons came when my wife said, "stop running" as I turned to exit an argument. The light bulb went off and I saw that rather than embrace conflict, I turned and ran.

My pattern of running did not teach me to know who I could be (strong, courageous, and open). Rather, this kind of strategy created the perception that others are the sole cause of my discomfort and unhappiness. Escaping the conflict, or ending the relationship, may only provide short-lived comfort. What happens the next time we face an adverse situation? What will we do the next time conflict arises? What if Dorothy continued to run away after being told of her family's love for her? What if she ran away from Oz? Dorothy's experience suggests we must look past our fears, develop a clear picture of what we want and then commit to obtaining it.

So much time is spent dreaming about a new life to be found over a rainbow. But it seems few commit to journeying into that foreign territory. When it's convenient, we see ourselves as dumb like the scarecrow, incapable of giving or receiving love like the Tin-Man, and afraid of owning our power like the Cowardly Lion. We become whatever we tell ourselves. Our self-talk is powerful and supports us in succeeding or failing. Imagine if Dorothy had stayed in her box during her journey to Oz. She would not have experienced the love of her new friends, nor would she have returned to her family with a new outlook on life. In fact, I will go so far as to suggest that Dorothy might have become the new Wicked Witch—oppressing others because of the dim view she held of herself. Can you recall a time that you thought ill of or gossiped about others? In that moment who did you more closely resemble: the Good Witch or the Wicked Witch? What was the result of your actions? Did you create, maintain or destroy your self-image? Did your relationships suffer? When Dorothy lands in Munchkin Land, Glenda asks her, "Are you a Good Witch or a Bad Witch?" What she meant was, "Are you a person of good character or bad?" How do you respond to this question? What defines your character? I define character as the sum total of all our habits. Other authors suggest character is who we are when no one is around.

The box can also represent other concepts in our world. For example, the state of Kansas was Dorothy's box. It is assumed that she never left the state. There are people all over the world who have never left their neighborhoods, cities, states, regions, or countries. The lack of exposure can be referred to as a geographical box. Keep in mind, that being in the box can bring about tremendous benefits. It's when it hinders our growth that it doesn't work. We can even find ourselves in a financial box, or we can create relationship boxes.

If we don't dream of traveling, managing (or making more) money, or creating healthier relationships, we can never commit to taking actions that will produce those results. Personal and collective growth is nurtured by continued development of the "self" through acknowledgement, acceptance and expression of who we are authentically.

DISCOVERY MOMENT:
- How many boxes do you have (2, 9, 25)?
- What does each box represent for you (family, friends, and strangers)?
- In what kinds of boxes do you place others (They get on my nerves, sexist, beneath me)?

CHAPTER 2
What's In Your Box?

And I am sure that God, who began the good work
within you, will continue his work until it is finally
finished on that day when Christ Jesus comes back
again.

Philippians 1:6

All of our life experiences are inside of us. Many of the
contents have been placed there by family, friends,
culture, society and God. In other words, there
are things that we've been conditioned to accept without
challenging. For instance, I can recall a conversation with a
teenage Asian girl whose family stopped speaking to her
because she was dating someone outside of her culture. I had a
similar conversation with a young man from India who didn't
want to participate in his family's tradition of pre-arranged
marriages. These are examples of people confronting the
expectations placed in their boxes by family.

I've provided a list of some of the contents I've discovered
in my box. Use this list to aide you in identifying the things
in your box. Definitions have also been given to support your
understanding of each example. Add your own responses to
each category. Commit to the process of identifying *what's in
your box!* Not everything in your box is bad or harmful. You

get to determine what things "work" for developing a healthier relationship with yourself and others.

Daily routines *(a regular, more or less unvarying procedure of daily life)* Going to school or work, doing household chores, driving the same way to and from a familiar place, getting up and going to bed at the same time each day, eating at the same restaurant, ordering the same dish from the menu, complaining about the same things everyday, reading the same kinds of books or magazines, hanging out with the same people, listening to the same radio station(s), eating at the same time each day, going for a jog or to the gym, calling friends, checking emails. ***What are your daily routines?***

Family and Personal traditions *(the handing down orally of stories, beliefs, customs, etc. from generation to generation)* Eating dinner together, going to college because your parents attended college, celebrating Christmas each year at a different family member's home, dating people both inside and outside of my ethnic group, adopting the same religious beliefs as my parents, respecting my elders, playing games or making crafts with my children, singing songs as a family while driving, not making New Years resolutions, volunteering my time. ***What are your family & personal traditions?***

Beliefs *(acceptance that certain things are true or real)* Marriage is forever, Going to college is the only way to get ahead, Men can be as nurturing as women, honor your mother and your father, all men are created equally, work hard and get ahead, Do the crime—do the time, "I'm not good enough," God exists, government is corrupt, your attitude determines your altitude, last hired—first fired, our society is sexist, one person can make a difference. *What are your beliefs?*

Assumptions *(anything taken for granted)* People probably will not like me, no one will speak because I am the new person, they'll never give the job to someone without a degree, people always like my way of doing things, if I say nothing she'll know what I need, we won't be friends because they look mean, they're too serious to have fun, s(he) doesn't look smart enough to know the answer, they won't care if I arrive late. *What are your assumptions?*

Criticism *(1. the analysis of qualities and evaluation of comparative worth; 2.the act of finding fault)* I don't like the way s(he) is dressed, she thinks she's cute, (s)he's not that good, anyone could do better, that person can't drive, a smart person would double bag my groceries so they would never break through the bag, that's just dumb, only dumb people drive slow in the fast lane, their opinions are stupid. *What are your criticisms?*

Judgments *(the ability to come to opinions about things; power of comparing and deciding)* These people aren't like my friends at home so I'll keep to myself, s(he) doesn't work as hard as I do, that country is inferior, or that person doesn't articulate their point clearly. *What are your judgments?*

Dependencies *(1. being influenced, controlled, or determined by something else; 2. relying on another for support)* Clinging to unhealthy, non-existent relationships (claiming someone is my friend who is not), relying on others to start conversations, needing others to introduce themselves first, never wanting to leave my block/community/state, parent(s), girlfriends, food, money, jobs, school, excuses, low self-esteem, sexual abuse and other traumatic experiences. *What are your dependencies?*

Successes *(a favorable or satisfactory outcome or result)* Good grades, new home, new car, increase in income, awards/recognition, new relationships, promotion, new friendships or maintaining old ones, college acceptance letter, learning the correct way to complete a certain task, saying "thank you" or "I'm sorry," sharing a secret, raising healthy children, marriage, joining a church, obtaining a new contract, starting my own business, serving others, someone acknowledging my support, people showing their love, demonstrating my love, participating in therapy, doing something new. *What are your successes?*

Failures *(a falling short or not succeeding in doing or becoming)* Sabotaging relationships, poor grades, not attending church, spending more money than I make, manipulating people and situations, speeding tickets, sent to court for unpaid rent, not graduating as expected, not taking notice of my weaknesses, not taking responsibility for hurting others. *What are your failures?*

Self-talk *(the inner conversations that we have with ourselves.)* I can do it, they are stupid, I want to leave, this is a long traffic light, "God, please help," I should apologize, I love me, I stink at this, this is too hard, I hate him/her, I love this subject, no one will ever know, things will never work out for me, I'm not good enough, I'm living my vision, I should stop and help that person, they should have their license revoked, I'm too scared to say what I really feel, no one loves/likes me, why is this happening again? *What are some things that you say to yourself daily?*

Emotions *(any specific feeling)* Surprise, sympathetic, thankful, paranoid, perplexed, prudish, lonely, guilty, dismal, curious, bashful, sad, frustrated, hurt, or happy. *What emotions due to frequently experience?*

Attitudes *(a manner of acting, feeling, or thinking that shows one's disposition, opinion, etc.)* The world is mine, I am a gift, I am significant, I don't care what anyone thinks, I'm beautiful, I'm better than you, or I don't care, whatever, my way or the highway. *What is your current attitude?*

Identity *(the characteristics and qualities of a person, considered collectively and regarded as essential to that person's self-awareness)* Committed, courageous, strong, respectful, kind, friendly, loving, funny, loud, quiet, shy, outgoing, humble, nurturing, protective, supportive, good listener, creative, charismatic. *What defines your identity?*

Relationships *(a continuing attachment or association between persons)* Mother/father, aunt/uncle, grandparents, godparents, friends, old girlfriends, wife, children, former classmates, teachers, clients, clergy, neighbors, God, myself, strangers, enemies, and the world community. *What relationships do you have?*

Knowledge *(all that has been perceived or grasped by the mind; learning; enlightenment)* Philosophy, meditation, psychology, math, grammar, computers, world issues, politics, business, literature, street smarts, religion, secrets, likes and dislikes. *What knowledge do you possess?*

Considerations *(a thought or opinion produced by considering that impedes our ability to succeed)* I don't have enough money, I'm too big, I'm too controlling, I wasn't born with a silver spoon in my mouth, I don't have enough education, I'm not skillful enough, There isn't enough time, I don't know anyone here, or I'm not smart enough. *Which three considerations due you struggle with most?*

Vision *(an image and a unique ideal of the future)* "Create a loving world where people understand their significance and live their vision," "...and wake up where the clouds are far behind me, where troubles melt like lemon drops, way above the chimney tops that's where you'll find me..." "One day sons of former slaves and sons of former slave owners will one day sit together at the table of brotherhood..." "I'd like to teach the world to sing in perfect harmony..." *What's your vision for the world in which you live?*

USING THE CONTENTS OF YOUR BOX

The box is the place we go to when our experiences frighten us or when we need to access the strength to risk or simply select the right "tool" for the job. When life is comfortable, our actions can be automatic. In fact, we may not choose to risk and go after the next dream or have a particular need met. It can be like having so much fun in the Land of Oz we forget or choose not to focus on getting home. We need to know when to click our heels and turn on and off our "auto pilot" switch. This automatic way of life has pros and cons. For example, on the pro side, a softball player will not have to think about how to swing the bat to hit a home run. This movement is a natural occurrence for her. She has practiced over and over and her response to the pitch is a by-product of tattooing, a process of the brain, and the muscular and nervous systems working together on a subconscious level to produce a desired effect. In short, the athlete reacts without conscious thought.

On the con side, we can program ourselves to automatically isolate ourselves from new people or tell ourselves that we do not deserve to fight for the good grade or the new job or a healthier relationship. We can even find fault with ourselves which renders us helpless. It is this stage of helplessness that prevents us from experiencing happiness and significance. The reason for looking into your box is to begin the process of deciding which things help you build a healthy self-image as well as supportive, nurturing, protective relationships. Once you get clear on the things in your box that don't work, you are ready to take the next step—looking at the things outside your box. We'll go over that in Chapter 3.

Given time, we can generate a list of things that we want: tithe, tell someone about abuse suffered, save $25,000, start a business, finish school, end unhealthy relationships, be less judgmental of self and others, make five more friends, become more confident, build a French Tutor style home, travel to Greece, create a world free from poverty and hunger, write a children's book, create greater intimacy, have four children… and the list goes on. The next step is using the things inside (and outside) our box to achieve those goals.

Dorothy's wish list included blue skies, singing blue birds, and troubles that melted away. Her entire journey demonstrated how she used things in her box and accessed new things outside of her box. What's inside your box? Keep your list of things "inside the box" handy. You will be asked to refer to it in the next chapter.

DISCOVERY MOMENT: *On a blank sheet of paper, draw a large box. Using the box-content categories above (failure, self-talk, emotions, etc.), write each word inside the box that you feel represents the contents of your life. Add your own words to the list.*

CHAPTER 3
What's Outside Your Box?

Seek His will in all you do, and He will direct your paths.

Proverbs 3:6

Dorothy made it clear that she desired a life that was fun, bright and full of possibility. She believed that she would have to go somewhere else (over the rainbow) to obtain this dream. Perhaps the rainbow was the bridge that she used to exit from and return to her box. Imagine Dorothy in her box peering over its walls into the land of possibility. Then, a rainbow emerges from her box extending beyond her walls into the great unknown. Dorothy must take action in order for her life to be different. Going over the rainbow is something new, a behavior not exhibited in the past. She was embarking on a journey—one of discovery. There were new people to meet, experiences to embrace and knowledge to gain.

I spent a lot of energy making my life look better than it was, but I didn't create new thoughts, behaviors or results. I merely altered the outward appearance of the existing ones. The results were still the same: I didn't share myself fully with others. I dreamed about an extraordinary life but never took action. I lied to myself about my unhappiness and spent most of my time and energy looking the part of a complete person but not being one.

In fact, I was great at looking good around others, being right about the way I lived my life and being in control of my emotions, relationships, and experiences. At least in my mind I did. For example, I believed that I didn't graduate from college in four years because my parents failed to pay my tuition. I believed my relationships failed because the women I selected had major defects. I believed my bank account was empty because no one would hire me or pay me enough. I constantly blamed others rather than take responsibility for what I could do differently. Like Dorothy, I ran away from personal responsibility. I too wanted to meet the great Oz and ask him to be responsible for changing my life. My personal growth and happiness was contingent upon someone else creating my reality, my meaning, my purpose, my destiny. This pattern of behavior was in my box, and I used it until the day I decided to stop running from the truth. When I became aware of how I controlled others and started taking responsibility for my actions, my results changed. I moved from pretending to be a friend to being one, from wanting to be a student to enrolling in a new school, and from complaining about not having enough money to quitting a job and starting my own business.

We all have the ability, at any time of the day, to move beyond our box. We must first think or believe that things in our lives can be different and that we have the power to create change. Second, we must step outside our comfort zone with only an idea of what is possible. For me, this is the same as stepping out on faith. There are no guarantees, but we know that staying in our box will not always bring about the change that we seek. Finally, we get to acknowledge our new discoveries (results).

Perhaps there is more than one thing to discover. For instance, Dorothy discovered that she had the power to lead others, the ability to create relationships and the will to overcome adversity. She possessed a vision that transformed the lives of everyone she met. The Munchkins discovered that they could once again sing and celebrate life. Dorothy's three friends discovered their own greatness. The Wicked Witch's guards discovered their freedom when the witch died. The Great Oz discovered that he could be himself and still be well liked. Dorothy discovered that the love she sought was with her all the time. All of these results occurred because Dorothy chose to risk, think and act in a new way.

We can all create extraordinary results. However, it will require us to risk and do something differently. Keep in mind, we will most likely not create "extraordinary results" every time we risk. Rather, it is through this process that we discover new *Thoughts*, new *Emotions*, new *Actions*, and new *Results* (T.E.A.R.'s). All of this new "stuff" provides us with an opportunity to change the way we view ourselves and others. Remember, before Dorothy left Kansas she felt useless and unloved. But when she returned to Kansas she spoke of friendship and love. Like Dorothy, we do not journey through life alone unless we choose to do so. Our discoveries mean little unless they are shared.

It wasn't until I acknowledged and embraced my disappointing results that I began meeting my needs. For example, I went from viewing work as an obligation to seeing it as an opportunity to serve others. In the early 90s, I worked for a science center in Pittsburgh. I had a negative attitude, and I felt the world owed me everything. In the first year, my performance was stellar. Then my bosses began to notice my "forget the world" attitude emerging. I began arriving late to work. I didn't complete tasks on time, and I even engaged in gossiping. I was placed on 90-day probation. Instead of holding myself accountable and responsible, I blamed the company for doing this to me. The truth was I was mad because I knew better and my boss saw past my "look good, be right, and be in control" veneer (ego).

After a couple weeks of being mad, giving everyone the cold-shoulder "victim" treatment, and making sure that my boss knew I had completed all my assignments because "she told me to do them," I shifted my attitude. I looked inside myself for forgiveness, responsibility, accountability and initiative and applied them regularly for six months. My results changed from being bitter, reactive, and somewhat productive to joyful, proactive, and incredibly productive. Five people had been promoted under my leadership. I created several dynamite programs; brought an empty science theater from an average of 12 persons per show to over 230 persons per show and increased the number of daily shows from 2 to 8; brought the issue of racism before the board of directors and had new policies created to address the issue throughout the institution, and was asked to participate on a national youth advisory board before being offered a new job in Maryland.

While my work life improved my interpersonal relationships were still suffering. I had not transferred the work skills to other areas of my life. Shortly after taking the new job in Maryland, I realized that I was still choosing to blame the world for my old and new problems. I was in a new setting, but I had quickly reverted to my old "victim" behavior of running from responsibility. I was way outside of my box and scared. This irresponsible behavior continued until the day I decided to end my marriage. That was the straw that broke the proverbial camel's back. It was time to identify specific behaviors that yielded undesirable results, and to examine my self-defeating thoughts. And boy, were there many. It was essential that I Substitute negative self-talk with positive affirmations and create new results through trial and error.

I was still messing up and messing up badly. It took some time for me to recognize my "unhealthy" behaviors. This was the first time I consciously looked at what I was thinking and doing. There were times when I didn't think I would ever breakout of my old habits. But I continued to embrace the process and press on. When I committed myself to write this book, I had to stop doubting myself and do it. In those fearful moments, I recall two high school students that said putting my words on paper would change lives. God spoke through those young ladies and their words pierced my fears. And so, writing this book is about focusing on something greater than my fears—and that's serving you.

Things will not change until you allow yourself to see something bigger than yourself and your circumstances. Begin acknowledging and embracing the things in your life. Everything that you have experienced is in your box, and it can all be put to good use. Begin looking for clues in your external world. Facing your fears can be challenging, but necessary for continued growth. An acquaintance told me to stop running when I experience fear. He said to take the second and third blows because the fear seems biggest at first. So, I'll say to you, "Stay in the fight." Commit to the process of identifying *what's outside of your box!* Remember, we have the power to create *T.E.A.R.'s* of joy or sadness for ourselves and others. Use this tool daily and focus on creating more tears of joy. So much of life is spent replaying what occurred yesterday or worrying about the next exam, paycheck or utility shut- off notice that we forget to embrace what is taking place now. The T.E.A.R.'s will hold your attention in the present. The beauty of this tool is that it's simple to use. Check in with yourself at any point in your day, week or life. Ask yourself: What am I thinking right now? What's my emotional state? What am I doing? How am I behaving? What results am I producing in this moment? Your answers to these questions will help determine whether you need to use a skill, talent or experience already in your box, or retool yourself for your present need.

I've broken the acronym T.E.A.R.'s into four descriptive parts. Definitions accompany each section to help you get started. Personalize the lists by adding your own responses to each category.

What's Outside Your Box?

Thoughts *(a result of thinking; idea, concept, opinion, etc.)*: I am significant, Everyone is a gift, I can disagree and still treat people with dignity and respect, I have something to say, I'll be proactive, I'll be supportive, I'll create fun in my life, I don't have to control others, It's okay to be wrong, I will apologize when I'm wrong, I will no longer prejudge people and assume that what I make up about them is a universal truth, I get to listen/speak more to others, I choose to be fun, open, and kind, I am the co-author of my life, I get to hold myself accountable for my thoughts, actions, and results, I am not my results—rather my results tell me how I am doing, I don't have to be right all of the time, I will meet new people, I will make more money, I want a career that looks like…, I want a house that looks like…, I don't feel like talking right now, This person is getting on my nerves, I want to scream, I'm hungry, Maybe I need to ask for directions, I think too much, It's okay to need the help and support of others, I am attractive, I love myself, I love others even when I find their behavior deplorable, See obstacles as opportunities. Visit my website (www.robertpruitt.com) there is a tool which will help you write a personal vision statement.

DISCOVERY MOMENT:
- *For the next 15 minutes, without distraction, write down everything you are thinking in this moment.*
- *List five new thoughts you want to possess!*

Emotions *(an affective aspect of consciousness; a state of feeling)*: fear, anger, joy, sorrow, lust, acceptance, anticipation, self-pity, disgust, kindness, pity, envy, discovery, confusion, surprise, wonder, happiness, courage, timidity, pride, shame, patience, relaxation, attentiveness, alertness, hope, despair, effort, interest, reluctance, respect, appreciation, love, grief, bitterness, terror, vulnerability, worry, rapture, ecstasy, hate, shock, remorse, peace, phobia, jealousy, modesty, loneliness...

DISCOVERY MOMENT:
- *Using the list above, write the emotions you experience regularly.*
- *List the emotions you struggle to express.*
- *Write the emotion(s) you are experiencing in this moment.*

Actions *(the way of moving, working, etc.)*: Say "hello" to people on the street or in stores, apologize to someone today, thank someone for doing something, ask a friend for help, buy flowers, listen to music, go to plays or museums, call an old friend, write a business proposal, sign up for an acting class, listen more/speak less, say "no/yes" more, take that trip to Africa or Paris, start that at-home business, start an organization, learn a foreign language, purchase new clothes, end or mend an unhealthy relationship, read a new book, write a new book, apply to the school of your dreams, be of service to others, seek to understand and then be understood, play games, pray or meditate regularly, share your feelings with yourself and others, seek win-win solutions, ask your boss for a raise, start a business, volunteer in the community, take a stand against sexism, paint a picture, take saxophone lessons, tap dance lessons.

DISCOVERY MOMENT:
List five new actions you will implement within the next three days!
(Example: I will call for tap dance lesson prices and times by 8pm tomorrow.)

Results *(anything that comes about as a consequence or outcome of some action)*: Establish closer ties with friends and family, achieve better grades, earn a job promotion, establish new friends, achieve greater intimacy, improve communication skills, create healthier self-image, select an appropriate role model, improve parenting skills, increase income, open up to possibilities, become more independent, turn visions and dreams become reality, provide a solution for ending racism, become more social, receive gifts that you never imagined, experience peace and happiness, develop self-confidence, reduce stress, become more creative, live in the moment, lead a simpler life, develop the courage to say "no," make better decisions, take responsibility for your life, accept feedback as a valuable tool for measuring where you are in life, dream more about what's possible, inspire others to go after their dreams.

Recently, I discovered the power of my self-talk. I had conditioned myself to solve all of my problems and even complain about life, people, and situations in my head. I would have private arguments with people who were not present. I would relive conflicts and traumatic situations over and over until I had sufficiently numbed myself with anger. Our though become our realities. Our thoughts are the words that become the program for the actions we will take. Our thoughts can help us clearly identify our emotional state or aid us in covering the emotion with statements like, "He's a pain in the butt," "I'm pissed off," "They get on my nerves," "I don't know how to feel," or "I don't want to talk about it." These statements do little to identify our emotions (See "Emotions" Chapter 2). Being vague or incomplete protects us from the need to fully experience pain. This protection hinders and delays growth. Imagine visiting the doctor and simply saying to her you don't feel well. When asked to describe the intensity of the illness and its location you respond, "I don't feel well." This vague response will delay and hinder the doctor's ability to diagnose the illness. So, there you sit for hours in pain complaining about the sickness and perhaps blaming the doctor for not helping. Now, let's shift. You take the time to identify the emotional pain (worried, fatigue, frustration) you experience and the possible causes (working two jobs, sleeping an average of 3 hours a night, being paid low wages, having no personal or free time). These clear thoughts provide you with the ability to make changes. Your thoughts are powerful! You create your reality with the words you speak and the actions you take. The book of Genesis begins with God speaking the world into existence. He has given us *free will*—the power to choose. Choice only takes place in the mind. It's deciding between at least two things. Take this time to look at the old and new results. Choose what you will do to transform one area of your life today!

DISCOVERY MOMENT:

- *List 5 new results you are committed to creating within the next week!*
- *Using the picture of the box, drawn in the previous chapter, write words around the outside of the box that represent your "new" possibilities (i.e., dreams, fears, breakdowns).*

CHAPTER 4
What's Possible?

Keep on asking, and you will be given what you ask for. Keep on looking, and you will find. Keep on knocking, and the door will be opened. For everyone who asks, receives. Everyone who seeks finds. And the door is opened to everyone who knocks.

Matthew 7: 7—8

Everything is possible when you dare to dream and take action! At age twelve, I spoke of traveling to Europe and Africa prior to getting married, driving across the United States, marrying at age 32, traveling extensively with my wife and then having kids. [Who knew I would eventually have twin boys?] Everything is possible, even telling myself I don't desire to have my dreams come true. My college years were rough: I dealt with my parents' divorce; I struggled to find work sufficient to pay my bills; I was repeatedly called out of class because of my unpaid tuition bill; I moved into new apartments each summer; and the list goes on. All of these experiences supported my bleak outlook on life. Additionally, my poor grades verified my self-declared stupidity (my Scarecrow), my fear of success highlighted my perceived weakness (my Cowardly Lion) and my unhealthy relationships proved that I was unlovable (my Tin-Man). I had sabotaged my dreams with negative self-talk.

However, six months after my separation, at age 29 I began living the expression "all things are possible..." New doors were opened: I traveled with two friends, in a tiny car, across America; I dated and socialized (typically I would find one woman and quickly start a long-term relationship); I initiated difficult conversations with family members, friends and the man that molested me at fourteen; I traveled several times internationally. Three years of committed soul searching (which still continues) led me to Sonia, my wife. I began transferring my job skills to my personal life and the rewards were tremendous.

Life was different because I regularly chose to risk thinking and behaving in ways that weren't the norm. Dreams (something for which there is no evidence) make a difference when you dare to follow them (take action). This is what Christians mean when we say faith must be accompanied by works. Each time my dreams became real, life became new and exciting. With each passing breakdown and breakthrough, I began to create a new picture of myself, a picture replete with strength, determination, pride, respect, joy, service to others, love, wisdom, assertiveness, and more dreams. As the picture changed so did the behaviors and the possibilities!

In the *Wizard of Oz* story, things were different when Dorothy returned home. The way she viewed her life was forever altered due to her "out of the box" experience. She discovered the power of living in the moment and valuing friendships. Dorothy even developed the mantra, "There's no place like home, there's no place like home, there's no place like home." Mantras are sometimes chanted and used for prayer, meditation, or affirmation. These statements demonstrate our beliefs or highlight a truth for us. Mantras are powerful self-talk tools that can have an amazing calming effect and simultaneously direct our thoughts and actions. For example, the Wizard had flown away and Dorothy thought returning to Kansas would not be possible. Then the "Good Witch" encouraged her to repeat the mantra. Dorothy became still, her tears subsided and she focused on her goal.

We can see that Dorothy's mantra has a variety of possible applications: 1) It might remind Dorothy to remain in Kansas the next time that she feels like running away from her experience, 2) "Home" could be a metaphor for Dorothy's heart and the mantra reminds her to love and respect herself, 3) "Home" could also refer to her physical dwelling, reminding her that her home is full of people that could provide love and support, 4) Additionally, it could remind her that she brings all of the experiences of living in Kansas to any place that she travels making a strange environment familiar and comfortable, and 5) It is possible that Dorothy's mantra serves to remind her to take care of home making it a place that is supportive, protective and nurturing.

In the previous chapters I mentioned that our thoughts evoke emotions, emotions dictate our actions, and our actions produce results. We never get to see Dorothy grow up and take action on her new found perspective. So, let's imagine what's possible: 1) Dorothy apologizes to Ms. Gulch, thus taking responsibility for her past actions; 2) Dorothy keeps Toto on a leash when they pass Ms. Gulch's home; 3) Dorothy's Aunt and Uncle build a stronger relationship by inquiring about and supporting Dorothy's hobbies and interests; 4) Dorothy explains that she ran away because she felt unloved, insignificant, and bothersome—a conversation that could possibly draw her family closer together; and 5) Dorothy discovers that purpose and direction (self-actualization) lie outside of her box, and she brings them inside.

Perhaps Dorothy's transformation, as presented in the story, has supported her in meeting all of her needs. Abraham Maslow's *Hierarchy of Needs* has five levels that move from basic needs to the highest order needs. Maslow, a scientist who studied human behavior, asserts that we seek to fulfill the need at the lowest level first, and only when those needs are satisfied do we progress to fulfill the need at the next higher level. Check out the descriptions of the levels below:

Level One: *Physiological Needs*—food, water, and air.

Level Two: *Safety Needs*—security, stability, protection, freedom from fear, freedom from anxiety, freedom from chaos, structure, order, and law.

Level Three: *Belonging and Love Needs*—friendship, love relationships, interpersonal (communication between two persons) and acceptance.

Level Four: *Self-Esteem Needs*—high self-evaluation, self-respect, self-esteem, esteem of others, strength, achievement, competency, reputation, prestige, status, fame, and glory.

Level Five: *Self-Actualization Needs* (Purpose)—doing what one is fitted for doing, self-fulfillment, and actualizing one's potential.

DISCOVERY MOMENT:
- *Which level best describes where you are in your life today?*
- *Using your box drawing, list the things, in your box and outside of your box, that you feel will support you in moving to the next level?*
- *If you see yourself on level five, list the things inside and outside of your box that will help you remain at this level?*

People experience success, significance and happiness at each level. Ultimately, it's when we are able to reach the point of Self-Actualization (level five) that we experience profound inner peace. Then, we are able to meet our needs while simultaneously living life with purpose and direction. People experiencing the fifth level regularly move in and out of their box keeping life fresh. Each level requires that we leave our place of comfort and take risks. Take my mother for example: she is a retired District of Columbia elementary school teacher. Formerly a pastor's wife and graduate of F.I.T (the Fashion Institute of Technology). She was clear about her calling to teach. Her position as a pastor's wife was demanding; however, it didn't keep her from acting on her passion to teach. Not even her excitement about fashion could steer her away from her purpose. The results Mom produced made it clear she was and still is living at level five. She is included in three editions of Who's Who Among America's Teachers, based on the recommendations of former high school or college honor students. Her multiple nominations put her in the upper 2% of outstanding teachers in America. She coached the 1993 State Geography Bee winner, sponsored by National Geographic Society. Her list of accomplishments is impressive. Each year, Mom took risks and reinvented herself so she could honor her commitment to serve a multitude of ungrateful students, countless demanding and arrogant parents and a cadre of envious peers. I watched her regularly fight back tears of frustration and anguish as she moved in and out of her box gathering the tools needed to serve. Discoverers, like my mother, understand that the box means nothing if its contents are not shared.

What's possible is that you not only change things in your private life but in the lives of people around you. Welcome to leadership. One of the greatest questions about leadership is whether leaders are made or born. For me, leaders are made in the image of God and born to serve others. Our leadership potential is inside of us and we need to constantly tap into it. But first, we need something to trigger our efforts. Seeds need water to trigger their growth, a light bulb needs electricity to trigger illumination, and an unfertilized egg needs sperm to trigger the process of conception. As leaders we need a cause, a conflict, or an issue we're dissatisfied with to trigger our stand. Dorothy took a stand for the "little people" who were marginalized, controlled, demoralized, dehumanized, abused, cast aside, and overlooked. Like Dorothy, leaders are willing to change the things with which they are dissatisfied. But changing the world only occurs when the leaders change. Mahatma Gandhi stated this best: "Be the change you want to see in the world."

Why all of this talk about leadership? Well, it's like the Good Witch waiting until the end of the story to tell Dorothy she had the power to go home (change her life) all along. Telling you that you have the power to make a difference in someone's life today might have fallen on deaf ears at the beginning of our journey. You may have been too preoccupied with what you needed, wanted or desired. However, now that we are at the "what's possible?" point, my hope is that you are even more open to looking at leadership as a way of life. Let me add this twist. When I speak of leadership, I'm really speaking of "servanthood." Leaders, which possess a servant's heart, are open and available to serve. They look at life in terms of what's possible not what's probable. If you know that the likelihood or probability of making your dreams come true is slim, you may stop trying. It's like the lottery: probability thinking will tell you not to place much stake in purchasing a ticket when there is a one in one million chance of winning. Possibility thinking suggests that at least one person is capable of winning and it could be me. Probability thinking will tell you sexism is here to stay. Possibility thinking will suggest that I can control my sexist beliefs and positively impact the people around me. Probability thinking may tell you the cost for addressing family issues is alienation and resentment. Possibility thinking suggests that a family member may have a breakthrough and healing may occur.

Leaders stand tall in the midst of adverse situations holding onto what's possible. This position isn't always favored by family, friends, and those we serve. However, it's the passion for achieving the image of what tomorrow can look like that keeps leaders moving forward, particularly in the face of adversity. Several years ago, I was contracted to provide diversity training for a local police department. The agency was under scrutiny by the Department of Justice for racial profiling and had experienced damaging diversity training two years prior to my start. The officers were angered by the public perception that all of the organization's members were racist; Now they were forced to participate in five years of mandated, "shove-it-down-our-throats" diversity training. So, here I come to share my gifts with no knowledge of the anger and hatred that awaited me.

The first year consisted of two four-hour trainings each day, five days a week for five consecutive weeks. I was in a hostile environment. With each passing hour I asked, "Why me? What am I doing here?" It became clearer that my vision to create a loving world where people understand their significance and take action on what matters would require me to jump in and out of the box. There were so many times when I wanted to run. But I believed it was possible that *someone* would understand my message and choose to apply it to their life. I left the training site on several occasions shaken, in tears, and asking myself if I was actually helping. It would have been easier, in the short-term, to give up the contract or disconnect from the members and present my material with little regard for their needs and emotional state. I wanted to let them have their way. But that's not how I felt deep inside. Something other than running away was possible.

My contract was extended for three additionally years. Each year consisted of 40 training dates. I never knew when, or how, hatred would show up, but I knew it would. Even after receiving death threats during the final year of the contract, I knew love was possible and that it would have to begin with me. Despite the numerous threats, I also received tremendous love and support. I was acknowledged by officers, in particular those who ran the training academy, for honoring my commitment and taking a stand for the members of the organization, and the citizens, who were experiencing prejudice.

This leadership thing "ain't" easy. Remember, it was the vision (an image and a unique ideal of the future) of freedom that supported African slaves, Jewish Holocaust survivors, and Native American prisoners in their fight to restore their humanity and create a life of endless possibility for their children. Change only happens when you believe that things can be different, create an image of what the future will look like, and then take action.

When you begin to live your life from the perspective that everything is possible, you will treat yourself and others with respect and dignity. Furthermore, you will see that everything is possible for those around you. The attitude is quite infectious. People around you look at the way that you live your life, especially in the face of adversity, and desire the same for themselves. Someone told me that we may be the only

Bible someone ever reads. Said another way, people will look at our actions and know if God does or does not have a place in our heart.

They want to be around you, seek your counsel, follow your vision and determine what matters to them. The Scarecrow, Tin-Man, and Lion all appeared to have greater confidence, love, and self-respect when they finished their journey together. Why? Perhaps after meeting this unlikely hero named Dorothy Gail it became clear that following her would positively impact their own lives without knowing why.

We all need someone we can trust. Someone with whom we share our deepest thoughts, someone who will support us in our quest to reach the fifth level—a person that will look beyond our faults and maladaptive patterns of behavior and see us as a gift—a friend who encourages us to think critically about how we impact others—a teacher that will remind us that we get to choose the values that we want to live by—a preacher that will share that all things are possible for those that believe—a leader that will remind us that relationship is a product of leadership—a stranger that will listen and ask, "what's next for you?" And especially when there is no one around, you get to trust and hold on to Gods' hand!

DISCOVERY MOMENT:
- *Make a list of five things you felt were not possible prior to reading this book.*
- *Make a second list containing five things that you feel are now possible. Feel free to move items from your first list to your second list.*

CHAPTER 5
What's Next For You?

Remain faithful even when facing death, and I will
give you the crown of life.

Revelation 2:10

No matter how hard we try to plan our lives, surprises
will occur. Sometimes we simply do not know what
the next second, minute or day holds. We refer
to our PDAs and day planners to get an idea of what's next.
However, they can't tell us what will fill the gaps between our
commitments. Change is always just around the corner. And
where there is change there exists doubt, anxiety, phobia—or
outright fear. Remember when Dorothy was about to journey
home with the Wizard and the balloon floated away without
her? In an instant her emotions swung from joy to despair.
Being left behind was not part of the plan. Now, how would
she get home? What was next for Dorothy? Sometimes the
best laid plans are often interrupted for a reason unknown to
us. If Dorothy sailed away in the balloon, perhaps she would,
once again, have relied on someone else to make her life
significant. It's also possible that she might not have discovered
her inner strength—her personal power [More on this later in
the chapter.].

Many people give their personal power away waiting for
someone or something else to determine what's next for them.

I know about this all to well. After telling my father about being sexually abused by a close friend of the family, I expected him to put his battle with cancer on hold to beat up the "bad man." Even as an adult, I wanted my father to fight my battle; to determine my future; to take control of my experience. Like Dorothy, at the end of the movie, I wanted to simply jump into the balloon and let someone take me away from my troubles. Many of us want what's next to find its way to us so we don't have to do any, or much, work. We want weight loss to occur without committing to a program. We want our boss to magically promote us without communicating the desire to take on greater responsibility. We desire open communication in our relationships, but we don't want to be vulnerable in the process. We want to win the Power Ball so we don't have to be concerned about our finances. Sorry to say, life is about working for what you want and embracing the process. And it will be a painful process. Our experiences pull and stretch us. And like lifting weights or jogging our bodies become fatigued. It takes time for the muscles to generate new tissue providing added strength. It's during this period of regeneration that we experience pain. We know the pain will end in time. Creating a mental picture of what you want the end result to look like helps to distract us from the discomfort. How can you lead others without a destination in sight? Imagine building a home without a clue as to what it will look like when it's finished. Sound familiar? Some of us are fearful of looking into the future and envisioning what's over the rainbow, so we use negative self-talk, the opinions of others, or fear to justify not dreaming or going after the dream.

What's next for you is up to you. It's about daring to pray, dream and then commit to making the dream a reality. What's next is a question that only you can answer. Your answer may be buried under your excuses and fears. Maybe the answer, or at best a workable solution, lies outside your box. Are you willing to peer over the protective walls and look into the land of possibilities? Take this moment as your opportunity to step up to another level. Declare what you want. Make it happen by keeping the faith when facing your fears. You will find it necessary to shift your thinking from time to time. Discover what works and what does not work with each new action. Decide to live with more memories (things accomplished) than dreams (things hoped for). If you can create a boring, predictable, ho-hum life, you can choose to create a lively, fun, service-oriented one. Take 100% responsibility for your life. Your mantra can be, "If it's to be, it's up to me." Recommit to your abandoned dreams. Grant yourself permission to live life fully. Be proactive. Be intentional. Be the gift you were created to be.

A few years ago, I sat in the living room with a former college classmate engaged in a six- hour conversation about her unhappiness. She revealed she'd been holding others responsible for her unhappiness. She had all of the evidence to prove how people had done her wrong. However, until now, she had not examined her contribution to that process. Using a house as a metaphor for her life, she eagerly began filling the rooms with possibilities. When we got to her "private room," she smiled while envisioning its contents: a French horn, Sterling Roses (which someone *else* had always purchased for her), green plants, a bay window seat, a place to pray, pictures of trips taken and no interruptions. Before leaving I presented her with a "life challenge" to purchase $15 worth of Sterling Roses by 2 p.m. the next day. Driving home, I replayed our conversation. I discovered that we had journeyed down a proverbial yellow brick road. The next day I called "J" at work. I could hear her smiling through the phone as she spoke of the roses sitting on her desk.

Taking the first step in a new direction can sometimes be difficult. Sustaining a new way of living can be equally challenging, but not impossible, especially when you invite others to support your efforts. When I decided to improve my friendships, I began by apologizing for being deceptive and dishonest. I went to one of my closest friends, crying and apologizing for not being truthful about the pain that I experienced during our college years. I also explained how I used him when I wanted company, but I was unavailable when he needed me. For me, our friendship was one sided, and I wasn't being respectful or considerate. I was a user by choice.

It was challenging to behave in a way contrary to my history. However, there were immediate benefits that support our relationship to this day. I continued my conversations with several significant friends from elementary and high school and college. Then I moved to my mother, father, step-dad, grandparents, cousins, and co-workers and bosses. I began creating a standard based on values by which I would live my life: honesty, trustworthiness, respect, concern for others, courage, responsibility, proactivity and accountability. I noticed extraordinary changes at work, in my relationships, in my family, in my self. My self-esteem was rising, and I was 100% responsible for the change in attitude and altitude! It was difficult. For each moment when I would stand tall there were dozens of moments when I would close myself inside my box.

I mentioned earlier that I believe it would have been harmful for Dorothy to have left in the hot air balloon because she was passively waiting for the "Wizard" to change her life. Because that didn't happen, I can only imagine Dorothy saying,

"I faced so many challenges and still thought I needed a 'man' to change my life. However, I was led to understand that I simply needed to trust in my ability to change the face of things!"

We will always rely on other people for support. That's a wonderful and necessary part of the human experience. But when we become co-dependent and neglect our own needs and feelings for the sake of pleasing others (which is more about seeking to please ourselves), our development is hindered. Many people become completely absorbed by a relationship and have no sense of self. They *are* the relationship. They won't think for themselves and typically consider personal responsibility an obligation. This was my reality. I only felt confident, happy and significant when my partner was happy. At least this is the lie that I told myself.

The changes I created in my life didn't happen alone. My friends, family, and even enemies, provided supported. They gave me a perspective about myself that I did not see, did not acknowledge, or did not want to see. Where I needed to be careful was in deciding if I was an active or passive participant in my development. As a passive participant, I waited for everyone else to rescue me from my situation and fly me home. As an active participant, I looked for options and selected what I felt worked best for the situation. For instance, it took almost ten years for me to stop blaming my parents and decide that I would handle my education. I depended on them to honor their commitment despite knowing they simply didn't have the money. The reality was, if I wanted to graduate, I would have to abandon my old belief (my parents would pay for schooling) and create a new one (it's my education, my life and my responsibility). I didn't like this new way of thinking and behaving because it was uncomfortable, but liking or disliking something doesn't alter the responsibility. As a parent, I don't always like changing diapers; however, it's part of what I'm committed to as a parent. Additionally, I don't always feel like conducting trainings or even responding to e-mails; however, it's a part of my calling so, I honor those commitments.

So, how do you keep going? How do you continue to "ease on down the road?" First, understand and accept in advance that you are not perfect and there will be occasions when you choose to hide in your box. For example, you may decide to talk to a friend about the way he dumps all of his problems on you, but you may stop short of actually making the call. This is the time to stop and acknowledge that you are not committed. Identify your emotional state—anxious, pained, and cautious and why you feel this way—fearful that your talk may cause pain and damage the friendship. And then risk and share all of this information with your friend. This unplanned conversation might sound like this: *"Mike, I am thinking about canceling our meeting today because I fear that talking about how I feel when you unload all of your problems on me might send the message that I want to end our friendship and I don't…"* Clearly, these are my words and they may not work for you. So, I invite you to act on the spirit of the example above and make it work for you.

Secondly, prepare for the times when you will take the easy way out. For instance, you may decide to cancel that meeting date and lie about the reason why. For the short term, you give yourself added time to adjust to an uncomfortable situation. But, prolonged avoidance could become problematic and habitual. Remember, our box provides us with comfort and shelter from the world. But, be mindful of the long term effects of staying in your comfort zone. Hiding can cause us to rely on isolation as a sedative, dulling our ability to accurately sense, experience and understand ourselves and our world. Many times we think situations will be worse than they actually turn out to be. We make up reasons for not taking action as a way to control the perceived hurt that comes with failure. But we'll never know if we don't take a leap of faith.

Thirdly, if you're tired of hiding in your box, recommit to one dream. Make your commitments measurable and specific. For example, "I will purchase $15 worth of Sterling Roses by 2 p.m. tomorrow." Rather than saying, "I'll get some flowers soon." Also, scale down what you want to do. Instead of making a special trip to the florist, order them on-line and have them delivered. Set yourself up to win! Break big tasks in to smaller steps. Dorothy wanted to get home but that required a multitude of smaller steps.

Lastly, less is better. You may think that you have more things to accomplish than time to do them. Prioritize! Go for quality rather than quantity. Be productive rather than active. We are all collectors of things but how many of the items collected really improve our quality of life? It's the quality of your journey that will bring greater rewards. Are you jumping from job to job or have you created the job or career you want? Do you have a lot of acquaintances and no friends or a few great friends? Do you create a lot of dissatisfying relationships or a few satisfying ones? Are you focused on limitations or possibilities? Are you problem-focused or solution-focused? Do you focus on serving yourself more often than others? Are you merely getting through each day or living with purpose?

The challenge that is outside our box can be as lofty as starting a non-profit organization with 50 Chapters worldwide or as tiny as purchasing a single Sterling Rose. It's about knowing what you want and declaring that the quality of your life is most important. How to make this happen begins with declaring what's next.

DISCOVERY MOMENT:

Declare one specific thing you will do within the next 24 hours that takes you outside your box and allows you to be of service to someone.

CHAPTER 6
What If Kansas Looks the Same?

Patient endurance is what you need now, so you will
continue to do God's will.
Then you will receive all that he has promised.

Hebrews 10:36

Each day, we can see something in a new way and behave differently. If you've read this book, completed the activities, and nothing in your life changed, I invite you to allow a week or two to pass. In this time, continue to honor your commitments. Sometimes we seek immediate results and when we don't get them we become frustrated and say, "This didn't help." Remember, this book is a tool for personal discovery and is designed to support your growth. But, it's what you put into this experience that will create your breakthrough.

I also invite you to reread the book or review memorable pages. Make sure that you are in a comfortable environment. Reading this in a time of crisis and panic may not be the most effective strategy. Revisit the pages of this book when you are relaxed and/or open to new ideas. Dorothy's enlightenment occurred because she was open mentally, and perhaps spiritually, to her experience.

In the mid-nineties I sought the guidance of a counselor. I needed someone to support me in arranging my life's experiences so I could begin effectively dealing with them. I wanted to make decisions that would move me towards the life that I dreamt about. During Dorothy's journey she received counseling from several people: the field hands, the Mystic, the Good Witch Glenda, and Oz to name a few. I have discovered that counselors can help you sort out your thoughts and create desired behaviors. You can also seek counsel from close friends who can objectively tell you what you need to hear, not necessarily what you want to hear. Select one or two people to talk to and share what you want to accomplish. In your sharing, you may discover clarity that didn't seem possible through merely reading. Remember, Kansas will not look different until you become the change.

Also, stay away from phases like, "That's a *small* change!" or "That's *only*…" or "That's *just*…" or "*No big deal!*" These are self-defeating messages that we internalize. And although we say we don't really mean anything by it, or we don't believe the negative things that we tell ourselves, our mind doesn't know the difference. Many times these messages unconsciously reinforce a negative childhood experience. Our mind doesn't make distinctions between what we *do* and *do not* believe. It simply records what we repeatedly say to ourselves and then tells the body to act accordingly.

The lesson here is: be mindful of the messages your feed yourself. Also, be mindful of messages others feed you. We can knowingly or unknowingly internalize these messages giving them power and the permission to direct our journey. My father would say, "You ain't gonna be nothing." Now, intellectually I know he didn't really mean it, but because of his influential role as "father" and "role model" his words secretly supported the negative view I held of myself. You may not create the results you dream about because you are unaware of your mental acts of sabotage.

There's no place like home when you learn to love it. Kansas is with you everywhere you go. If you want things to look different, you have to be different. Leaders, like Dorothy, don't always know how to create change. But their passion generates possible ideas until a workable solution is obtained. If Kansas looks the same, you may need to think a new way. If Kansas looks the same, you may need to identify and embrace your emotions. If Kansas looks the same, you may need to step out on faith. If Kansas looks the same, it is up to you to SHIFT! SHIFT! SHIFT! Imagine driving across the country in a car with a stick shift and you only drive in one gear? SHIFT! SHIFT! SHIFT! Remember, someone on your journey needs *you* to help *them* off their hook, to lubricate their heart and soul, or to remind them to courageously live a life dedicated to serving others.

CHAPTER 7
Things to Keep In Mind on Your Journey!

My unique spin on the story of *Oz* provides me with several symbols or metaphors that I will share with you. I have included my interpretations for each. More importantly, I've provided Biblical references so you receive the seeds of life. I hope you'll find them useful and applicable to your life.

The Certificate of Death marks the death of the Witch of the East. Give one to every excuse, bad habit, unhealthy relationship, self-defeating belief, fear, moment you doubted yourself or God, anxious moment, phobia, and lie. Effective leaders must be responsible.

> **Galatians 6:5** *For we are each responsible for our own conduct.*
> **Matthew 25:29** *To those who use well what they are given, even more will be given, and they will have an abundance. But from those who are unfaithful, even what little they have will be taken away.*
> **Ephesians 6:11** *Put on all of God's armor so that you will be able to stand firm against all strategies and tricks of the Devil.*

The Hour Glass was used by the Wicked Witch used this to measure Dorothy's life. Time is short. Live in the moment! Start living again today! Live your life with urgency. You will have to discipline yourself and be persistent about honoring your commitments. Effective leaders monitor how they spend their time.

> **Psalm 90:12** *Teach us to make the most of our time, so that we may grow in wisdom.*
> **Ephesians 5: 15—16** *So be careful how you live, not as fools but as those who are wise.*
> *Make the most of every opportunity for doing good in these evil days.*
> **Proverbs 12:24** *Work hard and become a leader; be lazy and become a slave.*
> **Proverbs 18:9** *A lazy person is as bad as someone who destroys things.*

The Haunted Forest represents things that scare you as you journey through life. Have the courage of a leader to hold steadfast to your dreams and walk through your fears.

> **Joshua 1:9** *Be strong and courageous! Do not be afraid or discouraged. For the Lord your God is with you wherever you go.*
> **Luke 12:4** *Dear friends, don't be afraid of those who want to kill you. They can only kill the body; they cannot do any more to you.*
> **Ephesians 6:11** *Put on all of God's armor so that you will be able to stand firm against all strategies and tricks of the Devil.*

The Flying Monkeys may be friends, family, enemies, and sometimes our own thoughts and actions that can weigh us down. Effective leaders identify and shake the monkeys off their backs by dealing with problems directly. Shake the monkeys off, and continue to serve others.

Psalm 119:143 *As pressure and stress bear down on me, I find joy in your commands.*
Psalm 86:7 *I will call to you whenever trouble strikes, and you will answer me.*
Psalm 55:18 *He rescues me and keeps me safe from the battle waged against me, even though many still oppose me.*

The Wicked Witch is a naysayer or jealous person that wants to steal your joy. These people tend to be oppressive and controlling. Don't let them steal your ruby red personality (the authentic-self). Sometimes *we* can be the Witch, which sabotages our lives and the lives of others. Effective leaders treat their enemies with compassion.

James 3:14-16 *But if you are bitterly jealous and there is selfish ambition in your hearts, don't brag about being wise. That is the worst kind of lie. For jealousy and selfishness are not God's kind of wisdom. Such things are earthly, unspiritual, and motivated by the Devil. For wherever there is jealousy and selfish ambition, there you will find disorder and every kind of evil.*
Galatians 4:17 *Those false teachers who are so anxious to win your favor are not doing it for your good.*
Luke 6:36 *You must be compassionate, just as your Father is compassionate.*

The Witch's Castle is a place that limits your mobility isolates you from family and friends, limits and controls your thoughts and suppresses your desire to live life to the fullest. Effective leaders understand that there will be times when they succumb to their humanness, however don't stay in the "box" too long because it can stunt your development.

Psalm 34:18 *The Lord is close to the brokenhearted; he rescues those who are crushed in spirit.*

Romans 7:15, 21 *I don't understand myself at all, for I really want to do what is right, but I don't do it. Instead, I do the very thing I hate...It seems to be a fact of life that when I want to do what is right, I inevitably do what is wrong.*

Philippians 4:6 *Don't worry about anything; instead, pray about everything.*

The Oil Can is used by love ones to lubricate you with words of encouragement. Communicating our needs to others stimulates personal and collective growth. You can't disclose everything to everyone all the time, so be careful! Effective leaders keep a cadre of people who will show their love at a moment's notice. Don't allow life to rain on your parade and cause you to lose your ability to move through life.

Proverbs 17: 17 *A friend is always loyal, and a brother is born to help in time of need.*

Ecclesiastes 4:9—10 *Two people can accomplish more than twice as much as one; they get a better return for their labor. If one person falls, the other can reach out and help. But people who are alone when they fall are in real trouble.*

Proverbs 15:22 *Plans go wrong for lack of advice; many counselors bring success.*

The Good Witch represents the people that tell you what *you need* to hear rather than what *you want* to hear. Warning! These are the people that we tend to push away when we don't want to hear the "truth" and resist growth. Don't forget to be the Good Witch for others. Effective leaders both seek and give wise counsel.

Proverbs 12:15 *Fools think they need no advice, but the wise listen to others.*

Proverbs 20:18 *Plans succeed through good counsel; don't go to war without the advice of others.*

Psalm 32:8 *I will guide you along the best pathway for your life. I will advise you and watch over you.*

The Poppy Field signifies our resistance to change. It can make us sleepy, lazy or lethargic. Watch out for the colorful words of people that encourage you to stay where you are. Some of these people may be "poppies" making themselves feel good by lulling you to sleep. Effective leaders master the art of self-discipline.

Proverbs 21:25 *The desires of lazy people will be their ruin, for their hands refuse to work.*

Proverbs 24:30—34 *I walked by the field of a lazy person, the vineyard of one lacking sense. I saw that it was overgrown with thorns. It was covered with weeds, and its walls were broken down. Then, as I looked and thought about it, I learned this lesson: A little extra sleep, a little more slumber, a little folding of the hands to rest—and poverty will pounce on you like a bandit; scarcity will attack you like an armed robber.*

1 Timothy 4:7-8 *Spend your time and energy in training yourself for spiritual fitness. Physical exercise has some value, but spiritual exercise is much more important, for it promises a reward in both this life and the next.*

The Ruby Slippers are symbolic of your authentic self, inner child, spark, spirit, personality, character or attitude. Effective leaders never leave home without it.

Ezekiel 18:5—9 *Suppose a certain man is just and does what is lawful and right, and...does not commit adultery....Suppose*

he is a merciful creditor…and does not rob the poor but instead gives food to the hungry and provides clothes for people in need. And suppose he grants loans without interest, stays away from injustice, is honest and fair when judging others, and faithfully obeys my laws and regulations. Anyone who does these things is just and will surely live, says the Sovereign Lord.
Galatians 5:22-23 *But when the Holy Spirit controls our lives, he will produce this kind of fruit in us: love, joy, peace, patience, kindness, goodness, faithfulness, gentleness, and self-control.*
1 Thessalonians 5:16-18 *Always be joyful. Keep on praying. No matter what happens, always be thankful, for this is God's will for you who belong to Christ Jesus.*

The Yellow Brick Road is your life's path. Your road is unique and highlights your purpose. We all have a path that we follow and it unfolds before us with every step. Your life's path is rich and full of potential and trials and tribulations.

John 16:33 *I have told you all this so that you may have peace in me. Here on earth you will have many trials and sorrows. But take heart, because I have overcome the world.*
1 Peter 1:6-7 *So be truly glad! There is wonderful joy ahead, even though it is necessary for you to endure many trials for a while. These trials are only to test your faith, to show that it is strong and pure. It is being tested as fire tests and purifies gold—and your faith is far more precious to God than mere gold. So, if your faith remains strong after being tried by fiery trials, it will bring you much praise and glory and honor on the day when Jesus Christ is revealed to the whole world.*
Jeremiah 1:4-5 *The Lord gave me a message…I knew you before I formed you in your mother's womb. Before you were born I set you apart and appointed you as my spokesman in the world.*

The Tornado brings moments of confusion or lack of clarity, when we feel ourselves spinning around. Clarity can spawn from confusion. Prior to experiencing a "breakthrough," or an "epiphany," we may experience a "breakdown"—feeling overwhelmed, pained, perplexed, puzzled, horrified, frustrated, or undecided. Relax and allow the winds of change to subside. Determine what you can control. Remember that Dorothy had to wait until the house came to a rest before doing anything.

> **James** 1:2-4 *Dear brothers and sisters, whenever trouble comes your way, let it be an opportunity for joy. For when your faith is tested, your endurance has a chance to grow. So let it grow, for when your endurance is fully developed, you will be strong in character and ready for anything.*
> **Proverbs** 27-12 *A prudent person foresees the danger ahead and takes precautions. The simpleton goes blindly on and suffers the consequences.*
> **Psalm** 37:7 *Be still in the presence of the Lord, and wait patiently for him to act. Don't worry about evil people who prosper or fret about their wicked schemes.*

Dorothy is the unsung hero, the ordinary person who creates extraordinary results through serving others. She represents the child in all of us who desires to grow, play, learn, teach and serve.

> **John** 13:4-5, 14-15 *So he got up from the table, took off his robe, wrapped a towel around his waist, and poured water into a basin. Then he began to wash the disciples' feet and to wipe them with the towel he had around him...: And since I, the Lord and Teacher, have washed your feet, you ought to wash each other's feet. I have given you an example to follow. Do as I have done to you.*

> **Romans 6:13** *And use your whole body as a tool to do what is right for the glory of God.*
> **John 15:13** *And here is how to measure it—the greatest love is shown when people lay down their lives for their friends.*

The Scarecrow represents our feelings of intellectual inadequacy or our fear of being smart a smart critical thinker that says nothing to avoid saying the wrong thing. It's a reflection of the people who are committed to being led by us as well as our own ability and willingness to follow others.

> **Mark 2:18-22** *And no one pours new wine into old wineskins.*
> **Isaiah 50:4** *The Sovereign Lord has given me his words of wisdom, so that I know what to say to all these weary ones. Morning by morning he wakens me and opens my understanding to his will.*
> **Ephesians 4:29** *Don't use foul or abusive language. Let everything you say be good and helpful, so that your words will be an encouragement to those who hear them.*
> **John 15:13** *And here is how to measure it—the greatest love is shown when people lay down their lives for their friends.*

The Tin-Man characterizes our inability to follow our heart, to connect with people, to serve and be served. This character mirrors our fear to love and be loved, to respect mankind and ourselves. It is also a reflection of the people who are committed to being led by us as well as our own ability and willingness to follow others.

> **1 Corinthians 13:4-7** *Love is patient and kind. Love is not jealous or boastful or proud or rude. Love does not demand its own way. Love is not irritable, and it keeps no record of when it has been wronged. It is never glad about injustice but rejoices*

whenever the truth wins out. Love never gives up, never loses faith, is always hopeful, and endures through every circumstance.
1 John 4:12 *If we love each other, God lives in us, and his love has been brought to full expression through us.*
Ecclesiastes 4:9-10 *Two people can accomplish more than twice as much as one; they get a better return for their labor. If one person falls, the other can reach out and help. But people who are alone when they fall are in real trouble.*
John 15:13 *And here is how to measure it—the greatest love is shown when people lay down their lives for their friends.*

The Cowardly Lion portrays our fear of owning our personal power, of being 100% responsible, a risk-taker, a leader, a courageous, vulnerable servant. vulnerable, flexible, courageous, wise and faithful. It is also a reflection of the people who are committed to being led by us as well as our own ability and willingness to follow others.

Philippians 4:13 *For I can do everything with the help of Christ who gives me the strength I need.*
Revelation 2:10 *Remain faithful even when facing death, and I will give you the crown of life.*
2 Thessalonians 3:3 *But the Lord is faithful; he will make you strong and guard you from the evil one.*
Luke 5:4-6; 10-11 ***When he had finished speaking, he said to Simon,*** *"Now go out where it is deeper and let down your nets, and you will catch many fish." "Master," Simon replied, "we worked hard all last night and didn't catch a thing. But if you say so, we'll try again." And this time their nets were so full they began to tear! Jesus replied to Simon, "Don't be afraid! From now on you'll be fishing for people!" And as soon as they landed, they left everything and followed Jesus.*
John 15:13 *And here is how to measure it—the greatest love is shown when people lay down their lives for their friends.*

The Munchkins epitomize the times we see ourselves as small and insignificant, not worthy of contributing to our world. In this state, we become doormats for the uncaring people around us. Additionally, "The Munchkins" are the ones we step on when we allow greed, jealousy, pride or self-centeredness to dictate our actions.

> **Proverbs 21:26** *They are always greedy for more, while the godly love to give!*
> **Matthew 6:19-21** *Don't store up treasures here on earth… Store your treasures in heaven…Wherever your treasure is, there your heart and thoughts will also be.*
> **James 3: 14-16** *But if you are bitterly jealous and there is selfish ambition in your hearts, don't brag about being wise. This is the worst kind of lie. For jealousy and selfishness are not God's kind of wisdom. Such things are earthly, unspiritual, and motivated by the Devil. For wherever there is jealousy and selfish ambition, there you will find disorder and every kind of evil.*
> **2 Chronicles 26:16** *But when he had become powerful, he also became proud, which led to his downfall.*
> **Romans 15:17** *So it is right from me to be enthusiastic {proud} about all Christ Jesus had done through me.*

The Aunt, Uncle and Field Hands portray the people who are closest to us and with whom we share the most and/or the least; They have an enormous impact on our lives providing feedback, direction and unimagined challenges. They may also be the ones who knowingly or unknowingly squash our dreams. These people, though close to us, may become the stumbling blocks that prevent us from sharing our gifts with others. On the positive side, they may be the ones who teach us about loyalty and community.

1 Timothy 5:8 *But those who won't care for their own relatives, especially those living in the same household, have denied what we believe. Such people are worse than unbelievers.*
Galatians 6:2 *Share each other's troubles and problems, and in this way obey the law of Christ.*
1 Thessalonians 5:11-13 *So encourage each other and build each other up, just as you are already doing. Dear brothers and sisters, honor those who are your leaders in the Lord's work. They work hard among you and warn you against all that is wrong. Think highly of them and give them you wholehearted love because of their work.*

Toto (the dog) personifies the quiet force which guides us towards our destiny. He represents the soft voice of a higher power that comforts us during a storm and praises us for our demonstration of faith. He symbolizes an opportunity to explore new paths, to experience new challenges and make new discoveries (our calling). *{You may need to see the movie again to understand the Toto connection more clearly.}*

2 Corinthians 11:26 *I have traveled many weary miles. I have faced danger from flooded rivers and from robbers. I have faced danger from my own people, the Jews, as well as from the Gentiles. I have faced danger in the cities, in the deserts, and on the stormy seas. And I have faced danger from men who claim to be Christians but are not.*
Psalm 32:8 *The Lord says, "I will guide you along the best pathway for your life. I will advise you and watch over you."*
2 Thessalonians 3:3 *But the Lord is faithful; he will make you strong and guard you from the evil one.*

EPILOGUE

So, here we are at the end of the book. Wouldn't it be great if this book solved all of your current challenges and unresolved issues from your past? I don't know when your breakthrough will occur; however, this moment of reflection will be one of many in your lifetime. My hope is that this book will serve as a spiritual companion as you seek enlightenment and purpose. After my father's death, I found a book about love given to him by a friend. On the inside cover my father wrote:

Enlightenment is an event; everything else is a process.

Welcome to your process. You know what your struggles have been. You also know what still holds you back even as you read the words on this page. Perhaps you will experience a blessing through your reading and will let go of just one thing today that hinders your growth. As I said in the beginning of the book, "Let go of your anger and be God's man," was my father's life-altering advice. And, I am telling you, 'Let go and be the person God created you to be.' If you don't let go, someone will not receive the gift you have to share.

Even as I write this book, I'm in the midst of another life-altering situation, which calls me to examine my T.E.A.R.'s. I'm realizing that my box changed forms over the years. Instead of a small box, which emits no light when closed, I've graduated to a "Pope-mobile-like" box. It is translucent, it provides adequate standing room, and it allows me to see what's going on in my world. And, like the Pontiff, I'm protected when inside. However, I will need to exit the box from time-to-time to physically connect with my world.

Life is never without struggle. These are the moments when God looks to support us the most. I also believe these are the character defining occasions for leaders—times when those around you will look at how you share and deal with life. Many times people will not notice the smaller challenges you face. But you can be sure you're being watched when you face death, separation, divorce, bankruptcy, a natural disaster, substance abuse and the like. And remember, God is always watching and monitoring your faithfulness.

I want to strongly encourage you to ask the Most High the questions you find difficult to answer. Like Dorothy, no one walks alone. And God will appear when you need him most. Sometimes He will remain silent to test your willingness to "keep the faith" and "press on" (continue to do a good work). He may remain silent so you can recall what He has already told you to do. Faith without works is dead and God wants you to work! Work on your relationship with Him, with yourself, with family and friends, and most importantly, with strangers and enemies.

Use the talents, abilities, skills and experiences you've been given for the benefit of others. Not everyone will like, love or appreciate the gift you are to the world. If Jesus could be crucified, Medgar Evers, Dr. King, and the Kennedy Brothers assassinated, shouldn't you expect to face some form of retribution, criticism or even death? Stand tall and continue telling your story. Stir the emotions of those listening. *Jesus told stories and he still invites us to find our place in them. What is your place in God's story? When did you lead people to their greatness? When did you lead them to their demise? When did you follow with clarity and conviction? When did you blindly move with the pack? When did you give up and close the lid on your box, locking yourself in and others out? When did you try to walk the yellow brick road by yourself? When did you let go and let God take care of your situation? When did you forgive? When were you vengeful? When were you nurturing and caring despite not having parents to model those qualities? When were you a selfless servant? When were you selfish? When did you cry? When did you laugh? When did you say "Thank you Lord I want more?" When did you last pray for help? When was the last time you shared your story? When did you last jump out of the box? When will you next share the gift you are with the world?*

While typing this conclusion, I was interrupted by a friend, calling from the ER, asking me to pray for her son who was just in a car accident and in serious condition. Today is Thanksgiving Day. Today is all we have. Tomorrow is not promised. Take action now! Here's a prayer I taught my three-year-old boys:

Thank you God for this day! AMEN!

I invite you to pray this simple prayer at the beginning and the end of each day. You'll experience greater joy when you are thankful for all the day will bring and has brought. God knows your situation and has promised to provide your "daily bread." Click your heels, open your box and let Him put what you need inside.

May the Lord bless you and keep you; May He cause His face to shine upon you and lift up the light of His countenance and give you peace now and forevermore, world without end—AMEN!

Bishop Robert L Pruitt

I leave you with this benediction that my father offered at the end of a worship service.